Impressions

BRIAN R. FROST

Published 2024

Printed in the United States of America

First Edition

ISBN (softcover): 978-1-963380-39-2
ISBN (e-book): 978-1-963380-40-8

For information, address:

Holzer Books LLC
8 The Green, Ste. A
Dover, Delaware 19901 USA

For information about special discounts available for bulk purchases, sales promotions, and educational needs, contact:

info@holzerbooksllc.com
+1 (888) 901-7776

holzerbooksLLC©

Contents

LIGHT

Tears in the sand as the sun begins to set
Behind the dusk, the long days of regret

A reflection in depth of the time that has passed
Never knowing the number of the ones that will last

An epiphany to sort as the memory sustains
A drizzle from heaven, cold as it rains

A moment in time to assess the cost
Finding pieces of self-direction since lost

The distance ahead guides the turn
A body of temptation remnants to burn

Scars to be healed in a time that is short
The pain from the loneliness still left to export

Making a connection in the hours that be
All this time right alongside me

A violet-blue as the shade settles to pink
The years with the sun both sizzle and sink

Essence in the air for one that seeks clarity
The breeze that cools the rushing disparity

Looking above for answers to stay
A peaceful calm in the skies of gray

Feel the colors vary from day to night
Behind the shadows of the dawning light

AFTER

How does one mend a broken heart?
Nowhere to look, to begin to start

The pain that comes from every beat
The soul is hurt and left to feel incomplete

How long does it take for the heart to heal?
When there is no emotion that one can feel

Will the pain at least ease in the days to come?
For I can only hope that there will be some

The thought of being empty is hard to express
When it seems that the heart is beating less

With each day that goes by, there is not much change
Except for the degree of emptiness left from this exchange

I look for you and to again hear your voice
Hoping someday that my heart will rejoice

But now there is nothing not even a sound
As I sit here wishing that you were still around

Another talk, another walk, another table for two
I would take my last breath to have that time with you

There was always a reason when you were around
And now the reason is short of profound

How long will it be before I can see you again?
When that time comes then my heart will win

I never knew until now about the word miss
As I long for your touch or a goodnight kiss

Maybe tomorrow my sorrow will ease
As I pray tonight, I will beg him please

One Percent

The subject matter today is the great people of our nation
It's hard to stay afloat these days with the anchor that is inflation

The heart of our country has always been blue-collar folks like you and me
It's extra tough to sit back and watch the road to entropy

Some say the two-party system is broken causing the divide to be much more
This thing is definitely out of whack and our values need restored

Our hard-earned tax dollars are wasted daily with the incessant bickering back and forth
Day and night around the clock, east to west, south to north

Everything is ripping apart and crumbling at our core
It seems like no one gives a damn about much of anything anymore

Our representatives breed divide and keep undoing what the other side has done
By the time each day is finished, nothing is accomplished so onto the next one

We spend our time governing issues that fundamentally do not matter
Watching our elected officials go at it sounds like a bunch of sophomoric chatter

It is the base of America that is feeling the brunt we are burdened to no end
Our infrastructure is falling apart but how many wars are we in

It's clear that no one in D.C is going to cut us any slack
It's about time that we the people take this nation back

You've had your shot you gave it your best you've done all you can you've said
We need a change from top to bottom to put this crap to bed

What is it going to take to focus on issues that help us to any extent
I can promise you that it won't be catering to anything that amounts to one percent

Bad News

The news can be depressing in nearly every way
Without honesty, there's not much left to say

Left and right are split down the middle
Why we have to be compartmentalized these days is another plaguing riddle

I grew up in a time when the news was an evening staple
Gathering as a family to watch it after time at the supper table

Now we are in a time where we can't believe what we hear or see
A far cry from when the news was an honorary trustee

I ask people today and find it to be a shock
Some say their most trusted news source is none other than TikTok

Bad news sells and keeps division on the rise
The outlets that we once trusted have paved the way to our demise

To sum up today's news with just one line
I could sure use more coverage of baby ducks and sunshine

REPENTANCE

I never knew the meaning of love until I found you
The words that you provide turn rainy days into skies of blue

When you find something to love more than you ever knew you could
An antidote for the heart that paces the flow as it should

Finding the things in life that have always felt undeserving
A blessing granted is a healthy dose of goodness in each serving

Letting go of the past is the first step to a new path
Finding forgiveness within yourself eases a self-appointed wrath

Absorbing what has already been done is a way to help you heal
Being all right with who we are brings a comfort that is real

Going through the mind is not for the faint of heart
Acknowledgment is the first of two steps and is the place we have to start

Time is of the essence the pain we have to let go
It's not an easy thing to do but a necessity as we grow

Acceptance is the other and is the harder one to swallow
Once we turn that corner the remnants are less that follow

Search for guidance within ourselves a solution on the way
The debt within us we will clear and no longer have to pay

Owning everything is just too much eventually we will fall
Leaving the pain behind us is helpful to us all

Take each second of the day treat every one of them as new
Seek the value in the moments ahead there are sure to be a few

Forgiveness is an escape artist and without it can be a life sentence
Find acceptance for the soul and begin the journey of repentance

MY FIRST FRIEND

We were five years old when we first met
With all the cards of life to be dealt yet

Friends we became, and soon we both knew
That through thick and thin our friendship would hold true

Countless days and nights through our youth spent together
Looking back now, there were no times of better

Good times and bad, no matter the cost
I can still hear you say... "It'll be all right, Frost"

From boys to men through life we became
But my feelings for you would always be the same

You brought me to Florida where I still live today
With all the thanks in the world, I could never repay

Though time and miles would come between us I'd find
Not a day went by that you were not on my mind

As I come home today to put you to rest
I can honestly say knowing you was truly the best

Our time together now may be over you see
But more time to come is destined to be

You can hear me now for this I know
So, until we meet again, I love you, bro

UNFOLD

The shades of gray that batter the mind
An imprint from yesterday in a moment we find

Time has passed, and more is to be
All in time, a faded memory

A collection of seconds that add to the pile
The more there are, the more worthwhile

Layered deep behind are the intrusive thoughts
Years of reflection to sort through or not

A lack of trust to feel incomplete
As an image of the memory engages to compete

The window to an epiphany can be a long fall
As the emotions are empty and no longer recalled

A desperate glance at the grace of perfection
A lacking example with the burning dissection

A piece of gray that fades with the night
From a distant view, it has vanished from sight

A tear on the edge as the hem works to hide
Only with a few are we to confide

An exhausting search leaves little to find
A reluctant hesitation to cohesively bind

A natural blue that blends with the gray
A fist full of colors in a hand on display

As the end of a memory escapes and turns cold
A lost sense of meaning begins to unfold

CHAGRIN

The prices at the pumps are up once again
The consistency in the inconsistencies is difficult to take in

Almost a dollar an egg at the local grocery store
I went to grab a carton, and my jaw hit the floor

There is no break at the pharmacy, but we have to press forward
One can see three others from the position in this corner

Everything is on the rise except for minimum wage
It seems to be a concerted effort to keep the bear in the cage

The quality of our output has diminished since back in the day
Another piece of our fabric lost along the way

Politicians don't work together and there is such a clear division
The worst thing a leader can do is not make a decision

The markets are a game that only people with money can win
Take it all out now before it bites you again

The war on drugs has been a complete and total disaster
Since it began the decline seems to have never been faster

Most have lost their manners and are quick to disrespect
Hiding behind a keyboard is a safe place from getting checked

The people of our nation are homeless and, on the streets
Sending billions across the pond a smile within the deceit

The highest office in the world has been a laughingstock for a while
The only effort that has been increased is finding more ways to defile

The greatest nation on the planet when it comes to freedom and liberty
Blinded by our own gluttony for everyone else to see

The hope is that one day we get it together and reel some of it back in
That looks to be a long way off much to our chagrin

THE EYES OF AN ANGEL

The eyes of an angel I see in my dreams
The eyes of an angel, or at least it seems

She never says a word, with her eyes that glow
Does she want something from me I do not know

I reach for her to take me away
But she looks at me as if I am to stay

Do I know those eyes from some other place?
Her hair, her skin, her beautiful face

I guess she will tell me when the time is right
Her peace, her calm, her warming light

I often wonder why she comes to me at night
Is it because I am calm in my personal fight

Was she sent to watch over me from high above
Or was she sent to show me in the absence of love

I wait to see her in my dreams at night
For she is truly the definition of a beautiful sight

PROFESS

A declaration needed for oneself
The dust has buried the surface of the shelf

Hidden in webs that keep it together
Impact buried, no value in treasure

The details lie in the back of the mind
A quilt of cover for no one to find

Discovery in light as it shines near
Kept at depths, beneath it stay clear

The moments are suppressed below a thin layer
Exposed in abundance in a cloud that is grayer

No words derived in the pause to the stare
Recalled in the memory with no one to share

A cold that beats above the under again
A notable difference in the time since then

Minutes remain with seconds to share
Outpace quickly a breath not to spare

The frayed ends are torched to burn
Between us two no need for concern

There in the distance not long do we feel
In a corner of the psyche a distant appeal

It lurks close by with no safety to find
An instant memory a path of decline

The haunting laugh is never far away
In the early years, it commonly stayed

Years of sorrow for all to confess
In the darkness behind the shadows profess

HALF EMPTY

A chill to cool the fire that burns
The tides between twist as they turn

A fix to taste a needle to nerve
Conscience absent at every curve

Blue to gray, darker to black
A loss in value to the top of the stack

The palate to quench the thirst for the cure
The grip from its fingertips, a bruised allure

A feeling ensues at a point in time
Lost in luster two nickels in a dime

Deep in the silence the depths of alone
A hint of guilt within the groan

A snap at the bend the sound heard before
Escape to the warmth the comfort to score

Darkened eyes a soul to dispose
A broken balance the lens can disclose

An anguished being left to repent
Tangled and twisted in the spiraling descent

A life in battle fighting the enemy
Lessons paid in full in the glass that's half-empty

THE THRILL

A tradition established before we can remember
The best time of the year is August through December

Taking the field after the spring game
To face an opponent that did just the same

The climate is changing, a new feel in the air
Saturday football for our country to share

The expectations are high for every fan
Hoping that this year we have a winning plan

Tailgating enthusiasts from locations far and wide
Wearing team gear with head-to-toe pride

Kicking off the season with kinks still in play
Better next week we think then we say

Orange on the stage with epic guests and crew
Saturday wouldn't be the same in a setting without you

The weeks press on with passion until the end
Cheering coast to coast for our very next win

Classic commentary to our ears from the tele
Iconic calls that include "Whoa, Nellie!"

Rivals in each division with heritage in full play
Hoping the conference championship will soon be on display

The air brings changes the colder that it gets
Fans rally together as victory proudly fits

The New York stage brings the best that's in the game
Some winners at the next level are in the Hall of Fame

The College Football Playoff has evolved from the BCS
Talent and teamwork are two ingredients of success

The holiday season brings friends and family together
So many great memories are made on a day that lasts forever

The season comes and passes with one winner on top of the hill
A seven-month wait before we can again relive the thrill

IMPERFECTION

Beauty is in the eye of the beholder
Near the iris, a sight of blue that is colder

A view to the soul gives the glance
Seeing in most the lack of chance

The closer we are to the color within
An in-depth look as the cover defends

A breath in without saying a word
Time within the vision is drastically blurred

A window that keeps the spirit intact
A pupil restricted speaks to the fact

Behind the retina a shade of fear
The closer we come to those that are near

Suspicion is clear in the white of the eyes
Learned through experience and the webs that tie

A glimpse to see what is coming to you
The absence of trust can be seen too

A penny for the thoughts that hide in the mind
With a lessened effort from the heart, we find

Lids cover the retina protection as we weep
A peek at a glance of comfort in a moment to reap

Vivid images help to see all that is meant
A life filled with worry a soul in contempt

The lens brings the light to the eye in a day
Shadows from yesterday are never far away

The eyes tell a story of ones that we know
Lost in a way outside of their glow

Healing in time to mend the connection
Pieces to be gathered in a life of imperfection

FOREVER

My love and admiration for you are easy to explain
You amaze me with your positivity between each drop of rain

Your modesty and style are in a class all their own
I never knew that love could nurture so deeply to the bone

An inviting smile that comes straight from the heart
You've been the warmth in the comfort since the very start

You've held my heart in your hands for the majority of my life
The purest blessing in my time is you saying yes to being my wife

I get lost in your eyes with each daily endeavor
You are still so captivating to me and I will cherish you forever

ONE DAY

They are all around us everywhere that we go
Important indeed but no place to call home

I look and often wonder asking the good Lord why
And every single time it brings tears to my eyes

How can this continue and be allowed to get worse?
Has the beating heart long since been buried fanning the flames of this curse

We all have a story from a time before now
We are supposed to be the best at everything but not yet this somehow

Some stay distant and can't look you in the eye
Others work quickly to look presentable smile and then say hi

We need assistance on a grand scale enough to make an impact
It is us that needs the help again no need for diplomacy or contract

An overabundance of things to fix how can this be so broken
Move quickly on this one my dear uncle please help us we aren't joking

So many have sacrificed for us and fought on foreign shores
Then only to come home and fight their biggest senseless war

We don't even know their names as they write on their new faces
Every single nook and cranny in all the familiar places

You print it at your convenience you know when it's for the team
How about the good old adage that once involved the American dream

Gridlocked over everything spinning our wheels for far too long
Same old boring song and dance out of tune is this hypocritical song

The older I get the easier it is to see all we do is line your pockets
We can't feed our starving people but hey check out this new rocket

I think we know now why it's been referenced as the land of milk and honey
Especially for all those good-hearted folks with handfuls of COVID money

Maybe one day when the stars align and the questionable votes properly sway
We can adjust our poorly sighted vision and lift a finger for our homeless one day

AROUND

Is it bothersome to your mind to hear the second's tick?
I count along, and to their minutes they stick

All the time to think: where has it all gone?
Behind us so quickly, with some memories that are fond

Math is so precise some clocks can be eerie
A matchup of perfection on a day that is dreary

So many devices created to keep track
On the back of one should be all that we can't get back

In each of its three elements only one matters somehow
At thirty-three percent that is this moment right now

Stay close to your family because they are all that you've got
When that phrase was coined time considering they were not

When all is said and done with not a soul to be found
Father time will still be counting with no one around

ANOTHER

The day finally came when we would meet our end
The soul is gashed from the loss of another friend

Love and loss are the two that bring us pain
Losing someone that you love leaves an emptiness that is sustained

The older we become less of the core can be found
Another piece torn ripping within the sound

Keep an eye on me until I can see you again
I will be yearning for that moment I assure you, my friend

Until

The sunshine is opulent in a perfect sky of blue
The prettiest things I've seen all day until the moment that I saw you

Keep

When the times get you down and you're feeling blue
Count on me to bring a smile to you

I'll recount the infinite qualities that bring the sparkle to your shine
Keep your head up and keep believing it'll all work out just fine

Little Voice

A furry teddy bear and a box that's chocolate-filled
Fresh plump strawberries and the bubbly's nicely chilled

Lingerie and lace with an insatiable appetite to share
A little voice inside me saying that's my kind of trouble right there

ALIVE

It doesn't take much effort to dull an individual shine
I mean, just because your opinion differs from mine

He doesn't like this and she doesn't like that
Today those are grounds for calling one to the mat

Not terribly long ago that used to be just fine
It's crazy where we are at this point in our time

Flags on trucks defiling God's people
May want to reconsider the church with the steeple

Could you imagine seeing that in the time of President Reagan
Not a chance in hell because the U.S. wasn't playing

The keyboard has stolen our integrity character and soul
Until the ugliness finally decides to take its toll

Casting stones has turned into throwing bricks
Let's open everybody's closet and see the dirt in each bag of tricks

Aggressive posturing like stance position argument or debate
About twenty-five years ago we would simply talk or conversate

Everyone is looking for someone else to blame
That doesn't matter it won't move the needle in the game

Take accountability and pride in what we do
Make a better world with respect between us two

Come together stand as one and together we will survive
Say your prayers sleep well tonight and spread joy while being alive

THE COST

The times have changed since back in the day
For the majority of aspects, I think most would agree to say

In the years when a handshake was as good as your word
Somewhere that's been lost and the fundamentals have since been blurred

A time when character was shaped in you from the first memories of being young
Now it seems that the initial step of the ladder is missing its rung

Humility and integrity were principles that helped you earn respect
Now with each new introduction, you really don't know what to expect

When the truth mattered and being honest sealed the deal
Each is by the wayside now and neither is part of what is real

Back when the basics were instilled in you with discipline as needed
Today our values have been compromised and in most have been deleted

It seems like the world has been set ablaze for all of it to melt
It never would have turned out this way if we didn't stop using the belt

We took the guidance out of schools about sixty years ago
It didn't take much effort for that yield to begin to show

As for the golden generations, it seems all the effort is now for not
When they used to work their fingers to the bone for everything they got

I miss the times when you could see genuine in an individual smile
The definition of that one has been misplaced for quite a while

Never before would it be acceptable for dignity to be dismantled
It wouldn't take much of a look to know what exactly needs to be cancelled

It's apparent today that in most the good has far been lost
Take a moment to look around no need for help in assessing the cost

EXCHANGE

A shift that occurs early for most, and for a few it never may
A trend that happens frequently and is a disruption to any day

A consequence of an action that leaves many with broken hearts
The foundation begins to crumble as the structure falls apart

You can hear the voices carry listening while alone
You can feel the difference in the air due to the deeper tone

The tears start to show as unanswered questions remain
Being pulled in many directions defines the inception of emotional pain

New faces appear as changes start to take place
Smiles converted to frowns as happiness vanishes without a trace

It's hard growing up when you harbor all the shame
It seems that no one else will so we must accept the blame

What once began as a lifelong investment
Has now turned into a damage assessment

It seems easier to move on and leave the broken pieces behind
As the events of yesterday are again replayed as we mentally press rewind

The whirlwind of confusion sets its path to rearrange
Everything seemed perfect until the implementation of this bi-weekly exchange

DIRT

It all began sitting in a sink
Out of a cold can was my first drink

Trying to fit in growing up to be cool
Chemically bound early the fool

The road ahead remained to be seen
In my teens, I colored with a new shade of green

A shaved lady the color of white
Adds to the seconds left in a night

A cold creamy yellow a candle melts the shade
Years of adversity before this would fade

For twenty years an inner sense to revamp
Designs multicolored pressed with a stamp

All the white coats lessened the thrill
A bottle to dissipate the drive-in ones will

The liquid flowed forever since that day with a sip
A life sentence suffered in its grip

The pigment of green is less harmful than all
To this day the stigma stands tall

The white in a blue on the wings of a dove
A heartbeat intense and too personal to love

An instant euphoria lands far from the top
Never before could one not stop

Nights accommodated with stars dimmed to low
Until the early hours the sedated rhythmic flow

The effects of the ink on the paper hand written
Broken in half and in no way smitten

The pressure that peers as we seek notoriety
Crushes the innocence that comes with sobriety

Experience will teach us no longer to flirt
The recap above the remnants of dirt

TRANQUILITY

The sky in the background is the color of white
Everything is beautiful when you are in sight

The feeling of joy that you bring to the picture
Always with me in my mind a permanent fixture

You hold on from behind with a ring on your hand
As we pause for the moment with our feet in the sand

The smile on your face with the wind in your hair
So grateful you chose me in this life that we share

The gulf behind us ripples as it rolls in
The timely cadence before it does it again

A glorious day when the year is about to close
The beauty is in the details a few freckles on your nose

I know without question that love is the purest thing
When I look into your eyes it's simply breathtaking

Beauty is a measurement both outside and in
Each second with you the heart beats again

A setting of perfection when you are with me
A recollection in memory a piece of tranquility

MERRY GO ROUND

A family waits for the local festival to come around
Lights and fun for all where laughter is a commonly heard sound

There should have been more studies before this next circus came to town
As the faces in our nation would take different shapes all with a similarly desperate frown

Many at first would find relief as given to help them deal
Another crosses the threshold of this frequently calculated pill mill

Early in the numbers was a staggering high-rising trend
One of those being the life lost of my very first friend

A design to assist with one intention in mind
Along with new ailments by the plenty we would begin to find

Two or three a day will help you with your affliction
Now without a Webster, you can define the darkness of addiction

Taking dignity and respect from our nation's patients since the start
Burying loved ones next to strangers now colder forever apart

Millions of lives have been lost while billions are being made
Dying in the streets versus made in the shade

The prices in the market compared to our neighbors abroad
An eighteen hundred percent discrepancy that screams obvious fraud

Another deception built to gouge the price due to demand
We are supposed to be on the same team not pushed into this quicksand

Everyday people need the output for their very survival
Scraping together pennies to meet the cost of this unforgiving rival

Having to assess each month as the cycle starts again
Will I be able to eat this week or will it all go to insulin

Rolling like a freight train creating a hot burning steam
No one is at the wheel as you crush the American dream

You know the old saying when people talk about karma
Can't wait until she comes back around and puts an end to Big Pharma

Listen closely and you can hear its creaking sound
As the button is pressed once again to start the merry-go-round

INTENTIONS

Some used to say it was going to hell in a handbasket
A quicker delivery would be in a hearse with a casket

The wheels are coming off and it's been this way for a while
I remember way back when that wasn't our style

People tearing each other down at the drop of a hat
We never would have thought of promoting that

The division is greater in every single way
We can hope but it looks as if it's here to stay

These days we can't even agree to disagree anymore
Never have we been in this situation before

Crime is worse than ever so keep watching your back
Don't forget about the threat of a cyberattack

We need someone to pound our gavel and call this thing to order
We should have built one a hundred years ago if we wanted a wall at the border

Man, I sure miss those simpler times
With a gun rack in the window of a Chevy and checking trotlines

In the days when you could count on a relative and friend
Idle chitchat at the pump until I see you again

People would say thank you and good morning at breakfast
There is no comparison then to these times that are reckless

When parents made the decisions and we lived by the golden rules
When things were taught with no agendas in local elementary schools

Social media opened the door to the threshold of dysfunction
Negativity and hatred fueled at every platform and junction

Nowadays most people just seem so hostile and bitter
Lashing out as characters in a fictional world known as Twitter

There are many things about the good old days that are still left to mention
I would go back in a second and trade them all for these times of ill intentions

Vanity

The exterior of the window is charred from the flames
The smoldering embers have exposed the shame

The spirit is broken less emotional flow
Representing the struggle from the events since sewn

The petals near the center are colorful indeed
The pulsating display with hunger they feed

From there another layer is woven and compact
Surrounded by questions the enigma intact

An inner circle is composed outside of the parameter
A contrast of blue is small in diameter

The degrees in distinction now all come to play
Despite the perception the guilty verdicts sway

The variables together help to solve the riddle
A spider on its back is in the shape of a fiddle

The envy in the concept is more than meets the eye
An addition to the mix that most can't deny

The elements to the wound are measured by desire
Kindled by the will for one to acquire

The sharpest of them all completes the connection
The burn to the touch the heat of convection

The dirt is swept away far from the door
The moral instability still yearning for more

The realm of darkness within the limits of sanity
Pushes to the interior the obsession with vanity

(My Call) P.S. Thank You Again ♪

Hello, I know it's been a while, and you know that'snot my style
I was hoping that we could talk, go to dinner, or just take a walk

I really need to talk to you, and I don't know where to start
I thought everything would be okay and then it all just fell apart

I know it's been a long while and I hope you're doing fine
It feels like such a big ask for me, but I could really just use the time

You've been there for me this whole time not faraway at all
I feel so bad that I left you and that's the reason for my call

I can meet you at the park bench you know the place we used to go
It'd really be nice to meet with you for a minute to say hello

I know I should have called sooner our talks have helped me down the road
I need to know if you can help me again but I'm sure I already know

You told me if I ever needed anything I could just give you a call
I need to take you up on that and spend some time with you is all

You've been there for me this whole time not far away at all
I feel so bad that I left you and that's the reason for my call

I need to feel your warmth again and you've always kept calm
You've touched me to my core I've just been away too long

Times have been tough, and the light seems barely dim
Not much has been going right and then it hit me I miss my friend

I really need you so much right now I love you .... Amen

P.S. Thank You Again

BE

A dark red in the water below
The deepest pain left to grow

A visceral burn broadly within
A connection between the depths of sin

A change that occurred one August day
A lost sense of meaning in the shadows of gray

The stabbing that frequents right above the hip
Repetition increasing lessens its skip

Right beside the heart a cold dull to feel
On the wrong side of the fence as a result of the deal

Every type given from home and across the sea
Took more dignity little left to be

In the right lower back there feels like a shank
Pain levels not scaled yet new faces to rank

The burning coals that lay inside
Like a bullet entered left to reside

The razor-sharp burn lives on the right
Front to back all day and night

Affecting physically everything to do
A wound left to breathe inside of you

Another loss is in the weight
Only with the scale can one debate

Been through the menu a hundred times or more
Pain on top of pain lessens the appetite for sure

Waiting by the minute for the process to heal
Emotions less an exchange from the deal

Every afternoon the lack of breath begins
A dose of humility from the highest now in

My heart is still with me her encouragement to me
Time together and the blessings that be

THE SCRIPT

This low is lower than I remember before
It seems that the goal is to settle the score

The inconsistency of the wax and the wane
Is more than enough to unbalance the reign

The thoughts most time bring the struggle it seems
With eyes wide open and even in my dreams

When will I learn that you are not for me?
Strike one strike two but not yet strike three

How can you be solicited with approval and ease
When a month with you brings me to my knees?

I want to pull away and call an end to this exchange
Through all the fog you bring that is not yet in range

Tearing me apart both inside and out
I beg and I plead but you're leading no doubt

It has been said to learn each and every day
For me that is simple it's always been the hard way

Breaking away as many parts start to roll
The biggest part of that is what's left of the soul

I've been splitting the instructions to get away from you again
This is our final round and one that I will win

BEHIND

A light blue sky with a cloud or two
The waves ease in with air that is new

The fluffy sand feels good between the toes
An offshore wind calmly blows

Palm trees sway both day and night
Possessing beauty within its light

Chutes open above dancing across the glisten
A breath is taken in for the soul to listen

The sun is high and its rays feel warm
Just a month in since the major storm

People a little south are still picking up the pieces
As it wreaked havoc on the West Coast beaches

The skyline goes forever as far as the eye can see
This view outside of the recent tragedy

He came and he went shaking the state to its core
Ripping apart the lives on the shore

The difference between both heaven and hell
A few miles down the road the story will tell

The scenery feels different as the breeze comes in
A desperate hesitation for the next one to begin

Decisions are being made to stay or to go
The beauty is less enticing for the ones who now know

The boats are sailing as the tide pulls away
Shattered dreams on a September day

A vast difference that miles can make
A path of precision left in its wake

The weather has not been better since he came and went
Disaster is a result of the first warning sent

A clear blue day and the sun with its shine
Visions imprinted not far left behind

THE SIN IN ME ♪

Through all my years of sorrow, you've kept me through the times
When my nights were darkest you blessed me with the light

When life had me down and things were getting tough
You brought me to the comfort that kept me looking up

You've filled this broken heart and washed away the pain
You gave me a fresh new start providing shelter from the rain

You've been here all the while every step of the way
It's been you all along that delivered me here today

You chose me to follow you all these things I know you did
You've helped me to tomorrow and the sin in me you've cleansed

I'm blessed to have this life and all the goodness that you provide
Not looking to the past no more in my soul, your will resides

I'll keep the faith in you with your mercy and your grace
I've been washed in the water and yesterday's been erased

I pray to you each night repent the dawn of each new day
Every second of every hour with you, I'll find the way

You've been here all the while every step of the way
It's been you all along that delivered me here today

You chose me to follow you all these things I know you did
You've helped me to tomorrow and the sin in me you've cleansed

PEACE

The warm feeling that runs within
An easier breath; a new cycle begins

Repetitive history is one element of insanity
This recurring theme scrapes the bottom of humanity

A cautious step to summon the will
Round in shape, the color blue is the pill

The comfort is inviting as it welcomes with ease
The initial release is a seductive tease

The vision starts to fade as the night comes to pass
The reassurance is brief not long does it last

The effects are clear as the mind starts to bend
The pulse is slowing as it works to amend

The elusive relief has been chased for some time now
Pleading for normalcy incrementally somehow

The numbing of the limbs is hard to defend
The intensity that it brings as the spirit descends

Another to cover a result that is real
The remaining attributes offer a lesser appeal

Sorting through thoughts is difficult to put together
As we battle back and forth during each endeavor

Here once more the cause and effect
Another assessment of deceitful neglect

The endless path that is blinding to see
A portrayal of emptiness described to a tee

The effort will continue the pursuit must increase
Hopeful to capture the fantasy and finally find some peace

THE BEND ♪

Another fork just around the bend
I need to decide which way to go
Take a right to find new meaning
And to the left, I already know

Trouble always seems to find me
In the corner where the lights are dimmed to low
Time's the only thing consistent
Gotta catch a ride for tomorrow's show

Her whisper always keeps me calm
She keeps me safe along the way
We made a pact a long time ago
That she won't take me to this place

Look to darkness to find the comfort
Behind the back in the shadows
A little more time to get it together
Just one more and then I'll go

Another day another dollar
Same old crowd again tonight
I guess it's time to get going
Gotta get ahead of the morning light

Her whisper always keeps me calm
She keeps me safe along the way
We made a pact a long time ago
That she won't take me to this place

Another fork just around the bend
I need to decide which way to go
Take a right to find new meaning
And to the left, I already know

This road's been long and I've grown weary
Different faces in the same old night
This glass is tall but the bottom's empty
I'm the only dog in this fight

TRACE

The faces in the patterns share a common view
They stare at each other with no contact between the two

The lines are incomplete no consistency within
The imbalance is evident and replicated to the end

They merge in the corner at the bottom of the structure
The bond that represents them is clear at this juncture

The finish at the top lacks stability to the right
This implication doesn't change from day to the night

The lines at the bottom bring shape to the pair
Others in the rotation eventually complete the square

Intentions can be noticed up close or from afar
The terrain at its midpoint is distinct with the scar

There is darkness in the perception in the angles of the mind
All of them can be mistaken with resolve to be unkind

A base in the elements hang long and upside down
A glance at its components resembles a frown

Light provides another window as new images start to peek
Finally finding the direction needed for the ones that look to seek

An impression in a moment from a frozen time and space
Now absent from the depths of visibility vanishing without a trace

FIND

The blanket of midnight lurks and begins to cover
All creeping things in the darkness are coming to be discovered

This frame of mind has been closed but often kept
Now released from the shadows the psyche comes to collect its debt

The loneliness is all around as you gasp to take a breath
The only thing in sight are the eyes of the face of death

Crawling through the elements on the elbows and knees
The past nips at the heels in the horror you are terrified and seized

You can't progress any further no matter how hard you try
It is now all-consuming and starts to close in on its prize

Fear is at every angle as it topples you in its wake
Despite the effort the haunting echoes of laughter shatter as you shake

The past is always close in the whisper of a memory
All the filth and ugliness retrieved so easily

The terror and pain are captured with little surprise
Assisting in the dissection of all the years of lies

Alone in the quiet, the panic is there right next to you
In the distance, the distorted figure has now completely come into view

The years of disturbances are hiding within us all
Many take them to the end of their rope and embrace them before the fall

The mind is fascinating it doesn't leave much behind
Keep the darkness under lock and key and pray for light to find

WHAT A DIFFERENCE ♪

We lost another good one yesterday
A brother on the line with few words left to say
It's never easy any time at all
The news of a final curtain call

Another time and another place
The details were in the smile on your face
The memories from the days in our youth
You know the innocent times and that's the simple truth

All the lessons in life and the time it takes
All the hearts along the way that break
You know the old saying well for goodness' sake
What a difference
What a difference a day makes

When the rainy days get us down
We need a helping hand to pick us up off the ground
It's in us all that we need to care
The love in a heartbeat's there for us all to share

The sun is warm it's fresh and new
In its rays, I can still feel you
We pick up the pieces to move on
And accept the news that another one is gone

All the lessons in life and the time it takes
All the hearts along the way that break
You know the old saying well for goodness' sake
What a difference
What a difference a day makes

One last salute to the times back then
A friend of mine since only God knows when
A buddy of mine from back in the day

What a difference
What a difference a day makes

MOMMA'S BOY ♪

Since birth, I've always been a momma's boy felt like a lifetime when I was young with all her joy
Looking up from her knees in my youth she taught me the values of respect and truth

A real good thing to be a momma's boy

You hooked me up big time to start the school years shining from head to toe would help ease some fears
And even though we couldn't afford em' you'd still come through with Jordan's

Feels really good to be a momma's boy

No, it ain't so bad to be a momma's boy you made it fun growing up with all you'd do
And you kicked my butt when you needed to no it ain't so bad to be a momma's boy

Time would change some things as it usually does the years became a little different was all it was
Yeah, some of those days were a little blue but, in my heart, my love still sat for you

And it didn't stop me from being a momma's boy

Raising other youngsters must be tough you've done it for thirty years still ain't enough
In your days you've touched so many lives some are still in school, and some are wives

My momma may have helped raise that little boy

There were probably many times when things seemed unfair, but you know your mom's a boss when she runs a daycare
I'm not real sure what all their folks do but they dang sure should be thanking you

You make me oh so proud to be a momma's boy

No, it ain't so bad to be a momma's boy, you made it fun growing up with all you'd do
And you kicked my butt when you needed to no, it ain't so bad to be a momma's boy

These days you're still a best friend of mine folks can call me what they will and that's just fine
Until this boy's time is through my heart like at first belongs to you

You make me oh so proud to be a momma's boy
You make me oh so proud to be my momma's boy

MEND

A rainbow appears below the sky ahead
A selection of color within its bed

A mist of silence in the clouds of gray
The end of a moment to begin the day

The water caps over to meet the shore
A calming breeze rustles in once more

A terrain of powder on the surface before me
At different depths in the deep blue sea

The cover breaks away providing no shade
Leaving appreciation before the complete fade

The rainbow has vanished until another time
Leaving a memory etched in the mind

Returning once again when the conditions are right
Nestled between the morning before light

The waves dancing in is the constant sound
In all directions, no one can be found

A time in a journey that has not met the end
A day in the mind a life on the mend

My Old Acquaintance

It's been some time since I've spent a day with you
The separation was something I felt I could never do

I see you every day everywhere that I go
Destruction comes in various shapes and sizes welcoming the ones that know

The warmth and comfort that you would once bring
Took an unexpected turn to a puppet on a string

Many days waking up you were the first thing on my mind
I am pleased with the progress of leaving you behind

I think of you and then you're gone in a flash
My only goal is for you to be a fixture of the past

Many nights with you and without the longer days
An entire lifetime spent drowning in your haze

I recently discovered the need to let you go
Something I did long enough was to dance in your show

When I was young, I was told you can look but do not touch
I wish I'd listened more, and the suffering wouldn't have been as much

One thing I've learned is that you will always be there
When it comes to you, I've had more than my share

Without you around there is less scheduled maintenance
In the rearview, I can now see my old acquaintance

MOVING ALONG ♪

I wanted to take some time
And say one last thank you
I'd never be who I am today
If it hadn't been for you

You filled the missing pieces
In so many lives
It hurts so bad now you're gone
But your memory shines so bright

I'd never have the means
To repay any of my dues
I am just sitting here buried
In the pain of missing you

All the laughs and all the tears
In all the ways that you'd provide
I can't wait to see you again
I'll see you on the other side

You'll be with me until my end
And I know that to be true
Until then I'll keep moving along
Cause that's what you'd have me do

I've always known throughout this life
That we'd all see an end
One could never prepare themselves
For a loss like you my friend

All the laughs and all the tears
And you filled this life with pride
I can't wait to see you again
I'll see you on the other side

You'll be with me until my end
And I know that to be true
Until then I'll keep moving along
Cause that's what you'd have me do

No Contest

I just joined social media and had no idea about the generational wars
There truly can't be any competition with the ones that stopped keeping score

Generation X are born leaders and weren't raised to be minions
We are still laughing to a great extent about your implementation of the ninth-place ribbon

We all remember the one-liners that our Boomer parents used to say
We need to revert back to many of those epic sayings today

The one that sticks out the most right now is what goes on behind closed doors
Looking at the world today that seems more applicable than ever before

Due to your upbringing, you feel entitled and seek to find reprieve
Not for anyone who's in a dress has a beard but their birth name is Steve

God doesn't make mistakes and Noah put two of each on the ark
If you haven't figured it out quite yet our bite is much greater than your bark

Go whine to the people who miserably failed you and continue to cry on their shoulders
This Xer has taken it easy on you and guarantees you the next one will be colder

You can combine each generation after us and you'll see who is the best
The results are blatantly evident and there is definitely no contest

ANEW

A moment to take in a day that has passed
Running on empty, the fumes never last

Time moves faster the older we get
As the days grow longer, we tend to forget

A minute to ponder a life of events
A deep dive it can be to a great extent

The second-hand moves to count the flow
Where all of it has gone it tells us so

The past is never far; that has been said
This time right now is the focus instead

It's there to remind us in a second of thought
Valuable lessons from experiences taught

Learn from mistakes to stay clear again
A life with many twists that will teach until the end

Recollection is needed to heal the mind
Time within a frame is never far behind

Each day gets better as we look to the hour
Yesterday is a beast and one that can devour

Now is better than the time before
Not that anyone is keeping the score

Keep focus in mind to balance the unsteady
Stay in front of what we know already

Better times to come take them in by the few
Looking ahead to a day that's anew

ROGAN

There aren't too many years that separate us in time
He has shared his legacy with the world and hasn't even reached his prime

A student of martial arts an addition to his résumé
His epic commentary calling the sport helped to pave its way

Some may not know, and others may not recall
In the mid-nineties, the fictional series he was in titled *Hardball*

The hit series that was known as *NewsRadio*
A few other comedy legends were cast alongside him in the show

Sometime later he was the host of *Fear Factor*
Another successful outing to include in one of many chapters

A comedic genius that brings many side-splitting laughs
Another tribute that needs to be included someday on his epitaph

His current show is listener-supported and one that is here to last
Teaching through effective listening is crucial to his vintage podcast

His guests are some of the biggest names in their game
He should already be inducted into the Broadcast Hall of Fame

He is the face of a generation that brings pride to be associated with
He is the man; he is a legend, and he certainly is not a myth

A well-deserved tribute from a regular fan
The world needs to give more credit where it's due when we can

A guy with firm beliefs that through his brand needs no slogan
A tip of the hat with respect and appreciation to the legacy of Joe Rogan

UNKIND

The weather is gloomy this early afternoon
A light sprinkle to begin the infancy of June

The thunder grumbles to establish the mood
A battle with nature a reoccurring feud

The wind rushes in with black in the distance
The leaves off their limbs with little resistance

Skimming across the ground out of sight in a flash
The light show makes an appearance with a ferocious crash

The rain picks up increasing the drops
Steady is the sound hitting rooftops

Overhead in an instant, a front is moving through
The scenery in the open is a chaotic view

The roar in the sky has announced its arrival
The fowl have taken shelter to ensure their survival

The temperature is rising to a noticeably warm
A large thunderhead now begins to form

The lightning within it initiates the dance
A mesmerizing experience leaves the eyes in a trance

The water in the grass is starting to stand
Close to the bay the thirst of the sand

Off on the horizon a contrast of gray
The forecast for tomorrow is heading this way

The umbrellas at the tables are leaning at their bend
Weathered by the storms and built to defend

The rain has lessened now to a drizzle
The fight in the events has begun to fizzle

Here and gone a crisp cool follows behind
A reminder of how the elements can often be unkind

BALANCE

The arrangement of color is consistent but lacking
The misrepresented stability is due to minimal backing

The form in the design is magnified and carried
In the corners, at a glance, the deception is buried

The perceived smiles are standard in a normal view
An instant response of desperation that is new

The warmth of the scheme is a captivating sight
The cyclical flow changes in the light

The spinning rotation is an invitation to the dance
The odd ones appear and initiate the prance

The spirit comes alive with a purposeful taunt
As the path from yesterday continues to haunt

The darkness on its edges highlights the strain
The void at the center as the conditions remain

The discovery of a notion that helps to take it in
Grab it quickly before it runs off the end

The clarity in value is aligned and then crossed
A lasting impression that can never be lost

The compass is near and well within reach
The prize of its worth in time it will teach

Endure the connection to keep the valiance
The direction is in focus to deliver the balance

MOMMA SAID ♪

I remember being young back in the day
All the really good things that momma would say
We'd have those talks while growing up
About life and work, you know, girls and stuff
I remember thinking I'd be blessed to
Find me half as one as good as you
I asked my momma, "How will I know?"
She said, "Son, she won't even have to tell you so"

Momma said she'll be
Sugar and spice and everything nice
Every bit of sweet goodness all rolled up inside
Like a PB and J with ice-cold milk
Soft as hospital cotton and as smooth as silk
Cuter than a bug as sweet as cherry pie
And she'll become the new apple of your eye

So, to all those mommas who raised us right
That kept us in line both day and night
All the whoop-ins that we made it through somehow
I'm so thankful for each one right now

Everything in our talks turned out to be right
Looking back now I just can't help but smile
I called my momma just the other day
To say the lady of my dreams came walking my way
Perfect from the heavens clean through and through
And I can't wait until she gets to meet you

Momma said let me guess she's
Sugar and spice and everything nice
Every bit of sweet goodness all rolled up inside
Like a PB and J with ice-cold milk
Soft as hospital cotton and as smooth as silk
Cuter than a bug as sweet as cherry pie
And now she's the new apple of your eye

When I think back to our talks back then
I just want you to know how thankful I am
For keeping me to the letter to make this boy right
Now I thank God for both of you each night

YOU ♪

I've danced in the darkness
Beneath the moonlight
I've been running straight ahead
Trying to make things right

I've spent my share of time
In an empty bottle
In a life that's been lived
Only at full throttle

And then I finally found
A way to start forgiving
And then you showed me
All the things that were worth living

I never saw so much beauty 'til I saw you
I never saw so much beauty 'til I saw you

Your glow is brighter than the sunshine
How blessed I am that you are mine
And your smile makes everything just right
You let the light in through the dark night
Seeing you is such a precious sight

I never saw so much beauty 'til I saw you
I never saw so much beauty 'til I saw you

Eighteen years gone by and we're still together
A love so strong like that it just gets better
The happiest day of my life is
When you said yes, you'd be my wife

I never saw so much beauty 'til I saw you
I never saw so much beauty 'til I saw you

Your glow is brighter than the sunshine
How blessed I am that you are mine
And your smile makes everything just right
You let the light in through the dark night
The sight of you is such a precious sight

I never saw so much beauty 'til I saw you
I never saw so much beauty 'til I saw you

UNIFIED

Looking out for each other seems to have lost its place
The emotions have been replaced by blank stares on the face

The joy and fulfillment that once filled the eyes
Has been overtaken by absence to no one's surprise

The overwhelming emptiness that this life can provide
Can turn one inward with a soul left to hide

The world around us can often seem so bleak
A misinterpreted meaning of turning the other cheek

Not being able to count on others like we used to do
Having that certain someone that you can lean on too

Most everyone seems to be in a world of their own
Everyone needs someone we can't go at it alone

Somewhere along the way, we have gotten off track
Empathy is just one thing that we need to get back

Between standards and morals, there is a definite division
A generational difference may have sparked this collision

It was once an obligation to lend a helping hand
We need an intervention to get our heads out of the sand

It's difficult to pinpoint when the importance of another was lost
We need to realize the damage and re-examine the cost

One thing that is absent in today's world that can't be denied
Is that we need to find the value in each other again and stay unified

FOR MY TIME ♪

Sometimes on the rainy days
The sun, she still will shine
Looking ahead to a day that's new
And leaving yesterday behind

Work to keep it fresh
For a feeling that's kept new
Every day is a steady reminder
Of the beauty that shines through you

I thank God for the sunshine
And for the cold in the rain
For calming down the storms of life
And bringing comfort to the pain

I thank Him for the starry skies
And the ocean deep and blue
I thank Him for everything
Especially for my time with you

You've been my best friend for a lifetime
My partner through and through
On the days that you aren't with me
All I think about is you

Reflecting on the time that's been
And the love that we share
All that we've endured
Has there ever been a better pair

I thank God for the sunshine
And for the cold in the rain
For calming down the storms of life
And bringing comfort to the pain

I thank Him for the starry skies
And the ocean deep and blue
I thank Him for everything
Especially for my time with you

BUFORD

A lanky-legged hound with manners in check
A warm feeling inside with a grin above the neck

Precision on the move poised when he sat
If dressed the perfect attire would be a tuxedo and top hat

A grumble in his voice when he wanted to play
A bit of joy we shared that I carry to this day

He'd get rowdy and talk then circle all around
The excitement in the moment the reoccurring sound

Trained to hunt to perform in the field
With a will to protect he provided the shield

His ears were floppy and tilted apart
An added ingredient a friend from the start

An eager demeanor mindful of respect
Love in the eyes is one of many ways to connect

Handsome as ever a ridge on his back
He would give me that look to slide him a snack

A large personality with humility he would shake
A relationship between two friends that neither would forsake

With an introduction to him, I definitely got a twofer
In my soul reminiscing the time spent with Buford

THE WAY

The road less traveled
Will still take you there
Make your own way
Leave nothing left to spare

The clock will always tick
Despite of what we fear
Clear out a new path
Be bound to shed a tear

The silence is often deafening
Yet the seconds sound so clear
Things are all around you
But the emptiness feels so near

I find myself always looking back
To the days that used to be
Thinking how it all came to pass
And the place that I lost me

The clock will always tick
Despite of all the fear
Clear out a new path
The fray will soon shear

Wondering about the time that's lost
And all the minutes that have past
Here today and gone tomorrow
None of this will last

The hands of time grind and turn
Back and forth to and fro
The hours have all piled up now
With nothing left to show

The clock will always tick
And time does sadly steer
Clear out a new path and make your way
For the end will soon be here

EASE

The disturbances have grown in this life
The deep cuts made from the blade of a knife

A metaphor to capture the feeling within
Each second of the hour repeated again

A chill to the sum of the eternal flame
Degrees of hollow a portal to tame

Finding the cause of what came before
A dissection is needed to heal the core

A willful abundance to seek the light
Lessens the shadows in the darkness of night

A silence in me nothing to feel
No emotions left for one to steal

Piecing together a soul that is lost
Counting the fragments mindful of cost

Direction to find a noticeable gain
Desired between each drop of rain

Looking ahead to release the past
Cleaning the wounds the total is vast

The shortest straw remains to be pulled
The arrangement of each can leave one fooled

The cold inside pierces the heart
Remove it first for a brand-new start

Picking up this flesh off of its knees
To make a stand with relative ease

When I Am More Than a Phone Call Away

Blessings in this life may seem to come and go
The times that we have shared are forever lasting as we know

Life will keep changing that's the one thing that's for sure
A friendship like the one we share can so often be the cure

Find the comfort in our time from an instant memory
I hope that'll bring a renewed smile to your heart so the world again can see

Think of what that someone might say to help you through the time
Reflecting on the ones that we have shared won't cost a single dime

Keep prayer highest on the list of all the things we do
Remember all the countless calls that ended with I love you

Keep the memories of the ones that have gone always top of mind
No matter the hour of the day let's recall them at any time

Always keep your head up as these times will try the soul
Forever know deep in your heart how much I love you, bro

Keep believing in the good Lord and keep looking up along the way
We'll keep each other in our prayers at night and request that He checks on you by name

I'll keep you in my heart along each step of the new day
These are just a few things we can still do when I am more than a phone call away

RAY

A white in the blue covers the sky
A feeling of comfort, the deeper the sigh

The sun is warm as it caresses the skin
An image of perfection a sight with no end

In body and spirit, the path is the guide
Feelings of wellness inward reside

Hope to keep the feelings intact
The adjustments made to stay on track

Impulse hidden can't be found to show
Nothing to tarnish the newfound glow

The sounds around disappear again
A pulse carries the heartbeat within

Selective choice on matters to speak
Scaling a mountain on top of its peak

A face is a structure its skin the terrain
Eroded years washed away with the pain

A moment to capture the silence around
Now not a peep a calm without sound

A soft breath in a pattern in the flow
Dedicated to the desire to grow

The peace in a minute filled once again
A welcome discrepancy between now and then

A higher look brings it all into focus
A better discovery a new diagnosis

The light shines through seizing the day
A piece of tranquility from a beam in the ray

UNKNOWN

A hint of innocence that deeply lies
No trust across the ocean that ties

Learned from the start to hide in plain sight
A reduced simmering risk for flight

Since the first day, the distrust begins
A vision painted from the hatred within

Learn to display a level of respect
Covering up the years of neglect

All effort made to lessen contact
Depleting the time there is to distract

No words spoken outside of the in
The distance in us is on display once again

The degree of difference so evident to see
The lack of consistency from you in me

A view of uncertainty still in your eyes
In addition to the perfect disguise

Secrets buried from a time before us
Covered and protected from generations of dust

Upfront and center with honor well earned
No stones remain left to be turned

From a red and white now with a blue
Another exception between us two

Eyes of duplicity a peer in the glance
The waters that divide us diminish our chance

Close to the end of this exchange
Sifting through ashes little remain

A front in play never to be blown
Answers to questions still unknown

YEARS GONE BY

And looking back at years gone by
I see those years deep in your eyes

Wondering how long our time will be
And how long before it's a vivid memory

Hoping that all that has been done is right
As I kiss you on the cheek each night

Words cannot express my love for you
It will never die for this I know to be true

I want nothing more than to hold onto you forever
But I know deep down that you are starting your new endeavor

I will be with you until that time comes
And you will be with me until my time runs

I would give it all away to have you another day
You have shown me more love than words could ever say

When the time comes for you to look down and see
I hope that you will keep a close eye on me

Maybe someday after we both have said goodbye
We can still look back at those years gone by

All the laughter and all the tears
That we have shared together through all the years

Right now, I feel that my heart is heavy
But I still have you to keep me steady

And looking back at years gone by

LAST ONE

The feeling inside is only caused by me
This feeling inside you've never cared to see

The things that I want the things I've never had
The only emotion of time lost is sad

Does it even cross your mind when it's eating at me
Life has proven that it is not to be

The effort that has been given has always been mine
Your effort has been lacking and with minimal shine

My feelings of sadness turn to anger it seems
Any glimmer of hope is losing its beam

Why am I the one that's left with all the caring
When it's with the rest of the world that you are sharing

Maybe the day will come when my caring is done
That will be the day when I take my last one

HOPE

There is still a glow on the days when it rains
Belief and perseverance are two that must remain

There are times in life that can often get us down
The inner peace inside us we must seek to be found

Reaching for the light that shines above us all
Once we feel its warmth, we will rise and stand tall

Love and will keeps the drive in us alive
Cherishing the seconds in each minute so that in the hours we can thrive

Not looking to the future or thinking of the past
Embrace today because it can escape us so fast

Lean on a loved one a family member or a friend
Hand in hand together until the sun shines again

Passion in the heartbeat keeps us all going
Throughout the energy, the spirit will forever be flowing

We must keep our heads up with a smile on our face
Dance to the sound of music with elegance blessed with grace

Keep moving forward and keep giving it our best shot
Love one another always with everything we've got

In life, there are many values to honor and keep in scope
Always keep the faith and never give up on hope

SOMETIME ♪

Last night I had a dream
Where I saw you
We sat down and spoke for a while
Like we've been known to do

We talked about the times that changed
And people we once knew
I still recall that look in your eyes
It's trust I've shared with few

Life is full of lessons
With good and bad times
In the end, we must change
It's how we all survive

Keep both feet on the ground
And head held high
Appreciate the talk, my friend
Let's do it again sometime

The next day comes around
The conversation's so profound
We talked about us and about them
For us and others this will be the end

Life is full of lessons
With good and bad times
In the end, we must change
It's how we all survive

Keep both feet on the ground
And head held high
I appreciate the talk, my friend
Let's do it again sometime

Nurturing Light

The depths of the darkness can be deeper for some
Hoping in time that the light will soon come

One can easily get lost in the emptiness of the night
Search for a beacon within yourself and emit it with all your might

The shadows in the dark can consume all of your space
Without the spirit of the light, you can never keep the pace

The path to the light is in the middle of your heart
It has always been it never left you never were apart

Rediscover the beam that in all of us shines bright
Find the peace and the comfort from the nurturing light

FOR HEAVEN'S SAKE

I remember a time when we could count on the news
And not lose any friends due to different views

When journalists had integrity and the truth wasn't distorted
When honesty was real and the facts were reported

Today most news sources are grotesquely biased
Separating the fabric of our nation that once tied us

Propaganda is on every corner and breeding uncertainty
Spreading disinformation as intended not inadvertently

It should be unlawful to fabricate and navigate false claims
Promoting such narratives should bring an end to the inept games

Once upon a time the news kept us informed while calming stress
Now it is responsible for widespread panic heartache and distress

Freedom of the Press is one privilege that makes our country great
But we need accountability and consequence in the media for heaven's sake

Milton Keynes UK
Ingram Content Group UK Ltd.
UKHW040844021124
450589UK00001B/265